T0368698

INSIGHTS INTO PRAYER AND AUTHORITY

IAN ARCHER

WestBow Press books may be ordered through booksellers or by contacting:

WestBow Press
A Division of Thomas Nelson & Zondervan
1663 Liberty Drive
Bloomington, IN 47403
www.westbowpress.com
844-714-3454

ISBN: 979-8-3850-3738-4 (sc)
ISBN: 979-8-3850-3739-1 (e)

Library of Congress Control Number: 2024922902

Print information available on the last page.

WestBow Press rev. date: 01/08/2025

PREFACE

Prayer is an essential part of the life of every believer, but it is often misunderstood.

While many have seen it as a means of 'making *their* requests known,' or making traditional recitations, true prayer serves a much larger purpose. It is the primary means by which God's will is done in earth. Although we can and should bring our needs and those of others before Him, what God wants should be our first consideration in prayer. Therefore, true prayer is about what God wants, not what we want.

If it is true that prayer has such a place of importance, then it is essential that we learn how and what to pray! It is not our intention that this short work should be a 'book of prayers', rather it is hoped that principles can be gleaned and insights given, that will make the prayers of the saints more effective, so that His "will can be done in earth as it is in heaven"!

May this work be of some benefit to the reader.

DEDICATION

As a child, I repeatedly prayed to God that my grandmother, Sybil, would have a long life.

This short work is written in the 103rd year of what she as described in our conversations as a "good life".

This is but one example of how God answers prayers!

CONTENTS

Chapter One

THE PURPOSE OF PRAYER

Prayer is a universal part of the human experience. In some way or form, on a daily basis, humans in every part of the earth, make utterances to someone for something. It is as natural as breathing, because it is something God created men to do! It seems as though we were hard-wired to know that we are a part of something greater. We intuitively know that we are subject to or need the assistance of powers greater than ourselves, at certain points in our lives.

In its most basic form, prayer is the making of a request or the seeking of the favor of someone in a position to give what is desired or needed. Interestingly, one may not have a relationship with or even necessarily believe in the existence of a deity in order to utter a prayer, because although it can be intentional and purposeful, many prayers are an intuitive reflexive response to internal pain or need and express a desire for relief or direction.

Much of the confusion that surrounds prayer is rooted in the consequences of the fall of man outlined in Genesis. In previous writings, we have stated that man is a spirit-being God created to have a relationship with Him. That relationship is a process that occurs in the innermost being of the person, so that when they have a need, want or desire that arises in their lives, it creates an inner burden that makes them want to reach out to the One that can help them. When a person is in a relationship with God, they will reach out to Him to help with or seek release from that burden. When they are not, they will reach out to anything or anyone they believe can help them in the spirit or natural realms. This is a universal truth, but also serves to highlight the fact that not all prayer is equal in God's eyes. The foundation of true prayer is relationship!

One may be in a difficult situation and utter a prayer to a deity or object for help and seemingly receive that help. The person will then put their trust in the thing or ritual that gives them what they desired, so that it eventually becomes a tool for them to get what they want. For that one, the act of 'praying' becomes an activity that caters to self. Unfortunately, that is not Gods desire for us, because the process does not draw us closer to Him but rather isolates us from Him and recruits us into self-service!

The Strong's concordance lists the following words and definitions of prayer:

(4335) Proseuche- is prayer addessed to God or a place for offering prayer to God,

(4336) Proseuchomai- to offer prayers, to pray (earnestly)

(G1162) Deesis- need, want, privation, penury; seeking, asking or entreaty to God or man

(G1783) Enteuxis- meeting with, coming together; a conference or conversation, petition

(G2171) Euche- a vow or prayer to God

The following definitions allow us to classify prayer into three basic categories: requests, communion, and what I call true prayer. Each kind reveals a different level of intimacy that is expressed through the act of prayer.

Requests are self-explanatory; a person asks for that which they need or want. This is the most superficial kind of prayer. The person, their need or the need of others is their primary concern. Of course, God may hear and answers these kinds of prayers, but He knows our needs even before we ask and is inclined to answer the need even before we ask, if it is in accordance with *His* will.[1]

---

[1] Matt 6:8

The other kind of prayer is communion. By virtue of its name, this prayer usually lasts longer than the request and involves spending time waiting before God. This is the kind of prayer that flows from having a religious disposition, or from a relationship with God. It is naturally more intimate, because it involves more than getting; it desires a sharing between God and the petitioner. It is most effective between God and the believer! Consequently, there is an exchange in dialogue taking place between God and man; it is a spirit to Spirit exchange, which is naturally more desirable to Him and more necessary for us! It is in communion that we can become aware of His will and can pray for His revealed will to be done. This is true prayer. It may be important to mention briefly the idea of intercession here. In Strong's concordance, the word 'euteuxis' (1783) is explained as meaning, in part, the petitions of believers as they fall in line with God's will. Consequently, any kind of prayer called "intercessory' prayer that does not fall in line with what God wants specifically, is not truly intercessory!

It is important to understand that while compartmentalization makes it easy to explain concepts, one can flow in and out of the different kinds of prayer. For example, one may be burdened with a need or concern and make their requests and while sitting there, they can start to commune; God's will can be made known and they can then embrace His will and join with Him in asking for it to be done in earth. Others may just make their requests known and go about their day. One is clearly more effective than the other is, because what God really desires is relationship, and what relationship becomes stronger without an investment of time?

We state again that the foundation of true prayer is relationship with God!

Chapter Two

TEACH US TO PRAY

... Lord, teach us to pray.... Luke 11:1 KJV

The followers of Jesus were conscientious Jews. They followed strict rabbinic laws, attended synagogue according to the traditions of their ancestors and prayed in the manner taught by their religious leaders. They did this from the time of their youth, not seeing much change in their lives or communities, but everything changed when the followed Jesus. They saw Him preach, teach and perform all manner of miracles with authority. They also saw Him leave them early in the morning to go off alone to pray. It was clear to them that Jesus had a different kind of relationship with God than any of the religious leaders of the day. He also had substantive and tangible results to back up what He was teaching. It is against this backdrop they asked Him to teach them to pray.

According to Strong's concordance, the word 'pray' (proseuchomai) used in their request, literally means, "to interact with the Lord by switching human wishes (ideas) for His wishes as *He* imparts faith." True prayer then is not a mere utterance of words, but an interactive process where man and God exchange ideas, with the goal that man would leave with Gods idea, as He imparts faith. This means that when a person comes to God with a list of their wants, needs or desires, but do not leave with His wishes or desires, true prayer has not taken place. Monologues ought not to be confused with prayer!

Their request prompted Him to teach them a *system of prayer* commonly called the "Our Father" prayer, and its rote recitation reveals one of the limitations of denominationalism. Its static structure rarely makes room for the dynamism of the living God. Many do not realize that Jesus did not teach them a list of words to recite, but a system of prayer for *those* disciples at *that time* based on where they were in God's redemptive plan on the earth. In fact, Matt. 6:9 quotes Him telling them to pray *like* this, *not* to pray this! His intention was to set a guideline for how they were to pray.

Consider that when taught this prayer, the disciples had faith in Christ as a teacher and miracle worker, but not as Messiah! They had not yet received the Holy Spirit, for Christ had not been crucified yet. Man's sin debt had not been paid nor had He risen from the dead to be Lord over all. It is with this realization that He taught them to say:

Our Father- this creates a paradigm shift in the way

they were to think of God; not as an unapproachable being afar off, but as their father. Until that time, God was referred to as Lord, Master, King etc., ideas that convey a class divide, as in a master/servant kind of relationship. Jesus was telegraphing that one day, they would *be* sons of God. Jewish thought at that time did not entertain such a view of God and the idea of God being one's father was blasphemous. According to Strongs, the Greek word for father (pater) used here means (among other things) one's creator, guardian, protector and one who has infused his own spirit into others and actuates and governs their minds.

As God *is* the father of *all* spirits it seems all the living, saved or not can call Him father.[2] However, it is when a person is born again and the Holy Spirit enters their heart that God as father takes on a completely new meaning. It is in this regenerated state that God is able to govern and influence the mind of the believer. It is in this new relationship that a believer becomes useful to God!

Who art in heaven- at the time of this prayer, God did not have access to dwell in the human heart. That opportunity only came after Christ's resurrection and the entrance of the Holy Spirit. It was on the day of Pentecost that the God who was far off came to dwell in the hearts of men.[3] Therefore, heaven alone is no longer God's domain, so are the hearts

---

[2] Eph. 4:6

[3] Jerem. 23:23

of men in the earth, when they believe.[4] As a result, it is no longer necessary for believers to recite this line.

Holy is your name- an acknowledgement of who He is. God alone is holy. This is why the honorific of 'Holy Father' that has been adopted by the head of a dominant Christian religion, wrongfully attempts to draw an equivalency between fallible man and a Holy God! God *alone* is holy and He alone is our true father; let there be no confusion about this![5]

Your kingdom come- is an acknowledgement that at the time, the kingdom of God had not yet come, while voicing a desire that it would.[6]

If we think of a kingdom as a territory ruled by a king and if we consider that after the fall of man in the Garden of Eden, God's influence in the earth through men was extremely limited, then, we can see the coming of the kingdom as God's intention to reinsert Himself into the domain of men. His is a spiritual kingdom, to be set up in the hearts of men. It cannot be witnessed in the manner of a political change of government, for the kingdom of God is within those who believe.[7]

After all, when Jesus appeared on the scene, John the Baptist was preaching that the kingdom of heaven (God)

---

[4] John 14:23

[5] John 17:11

[6] Luke 17:20

[7] Luke 17:21

was near.[8] By teaching the disciples to pray that God's kingdom would come, Jesus was multiplying the effects of *His* prayers on earth in that regard. Instead of one person praying that God's kingdom come, there were now at least twelve other people praying it as well!

Faith in Jesus' death and resurrection allows the Holy Spirit to enter the heart of man and they can commune there. That is why Paul teaches that the evidence of the presence of the kingdom of God is a relationship with the Holy Spirit.[9] With this being true, believers no longer need to pray for God's kingdom to come, for it has *in them* but they can and should pray for His kingdom to come in *others*!

May your will be done in earth as it is in heaven- it was and still is God's intent that His will be done on earth, in cooperation with man. This portion of the prayer follows the request for God's kingdom to come because they are connected; for how can God's will be done in the earth if men do not cooperate with it? Moreover, how can men cooperate if His will is not known in their hearts?

When Jesus was in the Garden of Gethsemane struggling with going to the cross, He acknowledged that two wills were in play, His and the Fathers![10] He knew what the Father's will was, set His own will aside, prayed for the

---

[8] Matt. 3:2

[9] Rom. 14:17

[10] Luke 22:42

Fathers will to be done, and then got up and executed that will. That sets the ideal for us all when we know what Gods will is and it also shows us what true prayer is!

God's general will is known through the bible when it shows us things He wants or does not want. For instance, in 2 Pet. 3:9 it states that "... it is not God's will that any should perish", therefore a general prayer would be that all men everywhere would come to the knowledge of who Jesus is and be saved. His specific will is known when He makes it clear to us what He wants in a specific matter or regarding a particular person. For example, we may be directed to pray for a person's healing, for them to have strength in a difficult time or other such matters. In order to be effective in prayer then, we must know what He wants us to pray, not only generally, but specifically as well!

Give us this day our daily bread- when Jesus was teaching his disciples to seek God's kingdom first, he made it clear to them that God cares about the needs of those who are His and He makes provision for them.[11] This now puts the modern day believer in the position of choosing to recite this part of the prayer as given or to use it as a place to thank God in advance for the provision He has already made as the good Father that He is!

Forgive us our debts as we forgive those who sin against us- this too reminds us of the state men were in

---

[11] Matt 6:33

before Christ's death. Their sin debts were not paid and this was an inducement to encourage them to be forgiving, so that they too would be forgiven. It reflects the 'an eye for an eye' mindset of the old law. This state was undone when Jesus died for our sins; thereafter, to those who believe, all of our sins are forgiven, for all time.[12] This does not mean that we cease to exercise forgiveness, it is just not for reasons those under the law would have done it.

Lead us not into temptation; but deliver us from evil- these two phrases go together and are reminiscent of Jesus being led into the wilderness to be tested of the devil. He knew that without the power of the indwelling the Holy Spirit, they could not possible hope to overcome the temptations the enemy could bring. He knew that in their spiritually infantile state, they would be fodder for the enemy, for he comes only to kill steal and destroy![13]

The passage below is found in Matthew 6 and is included for completion of the prayer:

The kingdom, the power and the glory are yours, forever- this is a declaration of the absolute supremacy of God in all creation. No longer would God be afar off, separated from man by sin and the controlling power of the enemy. Once Jesus accomplished His mission, who God is and what He has done for us and in us, would be

---

[12] Rom. 4:4-8

[13] John 10:10

displayed in greater measure in the earth and heaven, forever.

Therefore, in summary, praying a model prayer today would be different from that of the disciples when they asked the Lord to teach them how to pray. As an example, we could begin by still acknowledging God as our Father, for He is and we are His sons, and that He is holy.

We can acknowledge that He lives in us and His kingdom has come in us and we can ask that it come into the hearts and lives of others we may name specifically. We can ask Him to make His will known to us and to empower us to do that will.

We can then thank Him for meeting our needs for the day and then thank Him that our sins are forgiven. Then ask to learn how to walk in the authority He has given us by the indwelling Holy Spirit, to live above the power of the enemy so that we may not be ensnared in his plots against us, for the kingdoms of this world are become the kingdoms of our God and His Christ and He shall reign forever.[14]

There is no one way to pray, but instead of following the traditions of men or the rote prayers of denominations, one can ask the Holy Spirit to help them learn to pray impactful prayers, for that is God's will!

---

[14] Rev. 11:15

Chapter Three
ROGUE AUTHORITY

Behold, I give you authority to trample on serpents, scorpions and all the power of the enemy.... Luke 10:19 NKJV

Authority or power to act in a specific capacity is of two kinds, being either inherent or delegated. By virtue of God being who He is, all power and authority belongs to Him alone. He can act upon the dictates of His counsel in any capacity He chooses and none has the authority to question Him. That is inherent authority. Fortunately, He is righteous, just, and holy and only acts with pure motives. However, having all power and authority permits Him to give some of that to whom He chooses so that they can act under His influence, exerting that authority; this is delegated authority. Men however can act with less than pure motives.

The Greek word for authority used here in this passage is 'exousia', which refers to the delegated authority God gives *His* saints, authorizing them to act to the extent they are guided by *His* faith. The logical inference here is that the only people on earth who actually have authority to pray prayers that matter, or to exercise God's authority in the earth are those who have been born again! It is to them alone that He apportions power as He chooses. We also see that authority is not prayer, but it does empower and legitimize our prayer.

We have discussed previously that earth is the domain of man and it is God's desire that men cooperate with Him in bringing to pass that which He desires in the earth. This is consistent with a statement Jesus made about "*only* doing what He sees His Father do",[15] and "only saying what He hears His Father say".[16] These statements make several things clear, firstly, that there is a place in relationship with God where a person can *hear* what He says and *see* what He does as an indicator of what He wants to be said or done! When one does that, God's perfect will shall be done in the matter at hand, as that one cooperates with it.

Secondly, one must be at a certain place of spiritual maturity in order for this to occur and it happens by *His* faith. Jesus was able to distinguish clearly the origin of His thoughts, feelings and desires; He was able to discern what emanated from Him as a human clothed in flesh, and what came from the Father with whom He was spiritually

---

15 John 5:19

16 John 12:49

connected! How then can one truly exercise God given authority in prayer or any other matter, if one is unable to distinguish what originates from their flesh or the Spirit within?

Here we see an opportunity to pray for ourselves, that we may learn from God *how* to exercise the authority He gives, as He teaches us how to distinguish between that which originates from our flesh or His Spirit in us!

In the passage above, Jesus tells his followers, who do *not* have the indwelling Holy Spirit that He "has given" them authority, in the past tense. He had taken some of His authority and given it to them and He then outlined the parameters of that authority to include serpents, scorpions and *all the power* of the enemy. We see several things here, firstly, that they were already in possession of something, because of their relationship with Him, without being aware of it. One can have authority and be unaware of, or not know how to use it. How many people have genuinely confessed faith in Christ's death, burial and resurrection, are in fact born again, but because of the constraints of their denominational beliefs do not even understand what they have been given or how to use it?

Although the disciples did not have the indwelling Holy Spirit, they did have Jesus' instruction and personal example to guide them in exercising that authority. We see that authority had to do with restoring man's dominion in the earth over all the power of the enemy. Until this time, satan operated in the earth realm with impunity, doing whatever he wanted. All of the miracles Jesus performed and all of the sermons He taught were designed to do one thing, to help man understand that no longer did they have to be under the controlling power of the enemy. Not in their minds or bodies, for He had the power to make both whole; nor in their relationship with God for He wanted them to see Him as their Father. Nor over death, for He exercised dominion over that too. The one area in which God's authority was not to be exercised, was over other men. Whenever men seek to use the authority God has given them outside of the bounds of His will, they have become rogue.

In Luke 9: 51-56, a Samaritan village does not permit Jesus entry and James and John, offended by this, asked if they should call fire down from heaven to destroy the offenders. Jesus did not say that they did not have the power to do that, but replied that He did not come to destroy men but to save them. Here we see an example of the inclination to exercise rogue authority. They were given authority over the power of the *enemy* (serpents, scorpions etc), but they desired to use it to address a grievance against people. Here is a principle, the authority God gives is not to be used by men for *their* purposes, but for His, as *He* guides.

It is also important to understand that the authority they were given was over the *power* of the enemy, not over the enemy himself. There are many songs that have been sung, sermons preached and books written about 'tearing down' the devils kingdom, binding him and making him do all manner of things etc., when Jesus Himself did not do such things. Who has more power and authority than Jesus does and yet He did not "bind" the devil and cast him out of the earth, instead He addressed the power of the enemy at work in people through sickness, disease or possession, freeing them from his power instead! He came to seek and save that which was lost.[17] Throughout scriptures, even when the Lord or angels encountered the devil, their response to him was to simply say "the Lord rebuke you".[18] When believers directly confront the enemy without proper authority or a direction from God to do so, they have gone rogue, and who knows what misfortunes may befall them!

This brings me to the next point, when Jesus gave the early apostles authority He also told them that no harm would befall them. He sent them out two by two and they drove spirits out of people, healed them and reported all they did back to the Lord. They had no difficulties, were not thrown in prison or stoned. They were protected; no harm came to them! Notice how things changed when the Holy Spirit came and empowered them after Pentecost and how they rose up in new authority boldly declaring

---

[17] Luke 19:10

[18] Jude 1:9, Zech. 3:2

the gospel with signs following. In fact, the warranty on the authority given in Luke 10:19 expired with the impartation of the Holy Spirit.

Things changed because they were elevated from mere believers to whom *some* of His authority was given, to sons of God, indwelt by the Spirit, with the **same** authority Jesus had in the earth. They went from being spiritual neophytes to whom 'no harm would come', to enlisted soldiers in a real battle for the souls of men. A war through which the enemy would work through the systems he controls, to limit their ability to exercise the authority they now have as sons of God! This means that believers who seek to invoke the "authority" Jesus gave the apostles in Luke 10:19, are denying the new authority given through sonship and are attempting to appropriate something no longer in existence, to their detriment! It is the spiritual equivalent of sacrificing a sheep for your sins!

Within this discussion of authority is another area of great importance, as highlighted in the following scripture; Jesus said to his disciples in Matt 18:18, "I assure you: whatever you bind on earth is already bound in heaven, and whatever you loose on earth is already loosed in heaven."

Few teachings are more misunderstood than those of 'binding and loosing'. In the passage above, Jesus is giving instructions to his disciples about a number of issues that will arise in the life of the nascent church. He is trying to help them understand that He is giving authority to enable them to accomplish His work in the earth. One of the areas in which authority is given is in the area of 'binding'.

The word bind is the word 'deo' which Strongs reveals means: to tie, fasten; declare to be prohibited and unlawful. In order for a believer to make a lawful declaration that something is bound, they would have to have God's mind on it. They would have to know that He declares that thing unlawful and they are exercising His authority to make that declaration and to render that thing useless in the earth! Man is simply agreeing with and declaring in the earth, the will that God has already executed in heaven. Man is *not* declaring *his* own will.

The word loose is 'luo', and it means: to destroy, break, loose (so something no longer holds together) or untie, unleash, release what has been held back. Again, the believer has to have God's mind on this *before* they make the declaration that something is loosed or released. An example that comes to mind is in Luke 13: 10-15 of a woman bent over for 18 years that Jesus 'loosed' from her bondage. Jesus had the insight, first, to understand the source of the woman's problem and then based on the authority He had to destroy the works of the devil, He made His declaration that freed the woman from her bondage.[19]

Too many believers act as though the "power" and

[19] 1 John 3:8

"authority" they have is theirs to do with as they please. Nothing could be further from the truth and it is this belief that has resulted in so many abuses of power and erroneous teachings within the church! It has also opened up believers to attacks from the enemy *because* they are rogue! We must learn to exercise the authority God has given *within* the constraints He has determined, as His Spirit leads, and that will never happen if believers do not take time to sit and learn from Him!

Chapter Four

A WORD ABOUT FAITH AND HEALING

... by His stripes we are healed. 1 Pet 2:24

When Jesus was nailed to that tree (cross), so were our sins, and He became sin for us. It is our faith in His death, burial and resurrection that causes us to be saved from the consequences of sin, one of which is continued spiritual separation from God (death). The passage above gives us insight into another benefit of Jesus' sacrifice of His body to the beatings and scourging He suffered –we *have received* healing.

In Genesis 2:17, God commanded the man not to eat the fruit of the forbidden tree. When the woman and Adam ate that fruit, they chewed, swallowed and digested it. Its sinful essence flowed through their circulatory systems and went to every cell, including their reproductive systems, bringing death into it. That death created disharmony in the previously perfect sperm and eggs. Thereafter, whenever sperm and egg meet, it results in a new form of human life infected with sin. This is why every human born after Adam's fall, had the stain of sin and death in their physical body. This is why we age; this is why we die physically. This is why sickness, disease and defects manifest in the body.

Let there be no confusion, all disharmony that exists, both in the bodies of men or in the earth, are a direct result of Adam's sin. His willful act of disobedience to the command of God not to touch or eat from the tree, resulted in the entrance of disorder, confusion and the processes that eventually lead to death. For God created order out of chaos in Genesis 1 and Adam reintroduced that chaos in Genesis 3 through his disobedience! Therefore, God does not cause sickness, disease or death, nor should the afflicted entertain the devils suggestions that He does. If He did, why would He provide the antidote to sins effects in our spirits and bodies?

We must appreciate too that Jesus was scourged, *before* He was crucified. This means that God provided healing for our physical bodies *before* He provided the remedy for our wayward spirits! However, there is a vast difference between God's provision and our accessing that provision. Our spiritual salvation is not rooted in anything Jesus has to do, it is based on our accessing by faith that which He has already done. Physical healing, likewise, is based on what Jesus has already done, not what we believe He must do.

Often our desire to seek the things of God is rooted in our need. It is an intuitive realization that we are sinners in need of a Savior that sets us on the path to having an encounter with the Holy Spirit, who **reveals** to us who Jesus is. That revelation, combined with our faith and confession results in salvation. As it is written, if we believe in our hearts and confess with our mouths that Jesus is Lord, then we shall be saved.[20] That is the faith principle at work; that which we believe becomes real to us, allowing us to have access to something that already has been provided. As with salvation, so too with healing; one must believe in their hearts that they *were* healed by Jesus' stripes and confess that healing with their mouths, and it shall be so. However, why would one seek healing unless there is a need? The healthy do not ask for or seek after healing! It is because of the Lord's awareness that one of the ways the 'works of the devil' can still manifest in the physical body, is through sickness and disease, that he preemptively provided a remedy that we can access through another work He has already completed, His scourging.

This highlights another issue in the 'church'. Many have built ministries around the premise that you must be born again (saved), but that is only a half of what Jesus

[20] Rom. 10:9

suffered and died for us to have. Churches have missed the opportunity to teach and preach that Jesus died to renew your spirit *and* to give health to your physical body, and one can have both at the same time!

Why is this important? Because, when we are born naturally, we are pushed from one world into another, to grow, develop and mature. From the womb within, into a whole new world on the outside. As in the natural, so in the spirit; so that when we are born again, we are pushed into the spirit world as newborn infants to be taught the things of God and develop relationship with Him, until we become more mature sons. The problem is that if we claim our salvation but not our healing, then we can become mature in the former and be infants in the latter. Therefore, the protection God provided is inaccessible because one is trying to build their faith only *after* they have a need for healing in their body! Too many pray for healing *after* they are already sick! This was never God's intention, for Jesus came to destroy the works of the devil, both in our spirits *and* in our bodies! When our spiritual relationship with God is restored **and** our bodies are whole, only then can we take our place in the earth and exercise the dominion God ordained for us to have from the beginning, as His Spirit leads!

Therefore, when we exercise faith in Christ's accomplished work and confess for our salvation, we should do the same to receive the healing that was also provided. But why must one confess? When we confess that which comes by **revelation**, we instantly receive it. It is the revelation that Jesus is the son of God that secures the instantaneous salvation of our spirits with our confession. If however there is no revelation of a matter, then confession should be made *until* faith increases to receive that which is confessed. Faith comes by hearing and confession allows one to hear and increase their faith so that the physical manifestation of healing can come.

Imagine the following: nothing, a particle of dust, a grain of sand, a grape, a tomato and a pumpkin. Note that all of these are in an increasing size. Now imagine that they are each representative of different levels of faith. Faith can grow from being non-existent to becoming as large as a pumpkin, metaphorically speaking. So, if a person has no faith for healing, but they start to confess that which Jesus' stripes have provided, they can with time see their faith grow in that area. Now if the threshold of faith required for their healing is that of a grape, we can see that there are stages of growth necessary for manifestation. Likewise, if pumpkin sized faith were required, then the process of manifestation may take longer. This explains, in part, why some healings take longer than others do. It also explains why some may pray and confess but die before healing manifests in the body. Most of Jesus' healings manifested immediately in those He prayed for, because either He or they had the faith needed to access healing right away.

How much more then would we have to build our faith if we need healing, but we had not sought to access that which was freely provided much earlier!

May all the saints everywhere come into the knowledge that Jesus provided healing for both our bodies (by His stripes) and our spirits (by his death burial and resurrection) and both can be accessed, by faith, at the same time!

Chapter Five

PRAY WITHOUT CEASING

... pray without ceasing... 1 Thess. 5:17

We should consider that the instruction above was not given to an individual, but to a local body of believers. For how can a person, who has to eat, sleep, work, raise a family etc., never cease to pray? This verse highlights the importance of believers understanding that they are a part of a greater whole. It shows the importance of making prayer a part of their daily lives, for if individually we all make time to pray, then prayers will always be ascending before the Father to advance His will in the earth. People work, sleep, play and rest at different times that also means they will pray at different times, but if we follow the Spirits lead, the body of Christ in the earth will pray without ceasing!

It was stated earlier that it is not our intent that this would be a book of prayers, but this chapter provides a few examples of God's known will that can be fashioned into prayers for different reasons. In their private time, one can ask the Lord to identify areas He might want that one to focus on, identify His will in those areas and fashion prayers to suit!

PRAYERS FOR OTHERS

Consider the following passages below:

- It is not God's will that any should perish- 2 Pet. 3:9
- The Holy Spirit is given to those who ask - Luke 11:13
- He convicts others of sin, righteous and judgment- John 16:8
- It is the Father that draws people to Jesus- John 6:44

If fashioning a prayer for an unsaved person, for example, one can use the passages above (or others as well) like this:

"Father, it is not your will that _____ would die without knowing you. Please convict them of the sin in their lives, the judgment to come and give them a desire for righteousness. Draw them to Jesus, for only You can do that, give them your Holy Spirit and let your kingdom come in their heart and life. Amen.

In areas where God's revealed will (through communion) is unknown, the bible can give direction into God's will or His desires for many other aspects of our lives. One can then identify the need and pray His will for others in those areas, in the same manner as well.

PRAYER FOR BELIEVERS

Jesus prayed in John 17: 20-26 that believers would be one even as He and the Father are one. There is one Holy Spirit and He has one mind. The reality of denominationalism reveals that there has not been much success in the area of oneness. Denominations arise because people mix *their* mind, *their* biases or inspiration received from other spirits, with that which may have originated in the Spirit. They then build fortifications around their doctrinal positions. How else can so many 'churches' claiming to be "Christian" have so many different minds? Is this not contrary to the unity that the Spirit wants?

Institutions called 'churches' are filled with people in leadership positions and the pews, who are not even saved! They are excellent ambassadors for their religion, but they have no relationship with God and know nothing of His kingdom or what He wants. They have secularized the 'church', having a form of godliness while denying its power.[21] Therefore, it is essential in this day that likeminded people, with faith in God, would pray that those who believe in Christ would be one in a way that allows God to use them in the way He wants to. This means one's allegiance is not to a religion or a system of beliefs that people in a building use in place of God's direction. We first need to identify those who are committed to and in relationship with Him. For it is these ones who are the true church! It is they, who are connected in spirit, even if there is no physical building! How can the true church (body of Christ in the earth) be effective if the body is dismembered and scattered far and wide?

He has given different believers gifts, abilities and roles in building *His* church for one purpose, to advance His kingdom in the earth.[22] When the mouth, eye, hand and feet are disjointed, people may build their personal fiefdoms and have the appearance of individual success, but the kingdom suffers, God's will is not advanced and the works of the devil are not destroyed![23] Ephesians 4:11-16 highlights this very point; maturity in the things of the spirit makes the church more effective, productive and unified in purpose.

Pray that believers everywhere would be one in spirit; that they would be more faithful to God and the

---

[21] 2 Tim, 3:5

[22] Eph. 4:12

[23] Eph 4:16

fulfilling His purposes. Pray that they would be prepared to put their ambitions, biases and traditions aside. For denominationalism will see its end when the Spirit is able to unite and bind believers together with peace so that there is *one* Lord, *one* faith and *one* baptism![24]

PRAYERS FOR SELF

We should not neglect praying for ourselves. Among the many things that can be prayed are:

- The eyes of our understanding would be enlightened: Eph. 1:18
- That we would delight to do His will: Psalm 40:8
- That we would not fall into temptation: Matt. 26: 41
- That He would keep us from falling: Jude 1:24
- That we would come into the fullness of who we are meant to be as sons of God: Eph. 4:13

There is no end to the things we can pray for ourselves. Believers need to know the truth of who they, are what they are meant to do in the earth and they need strategies for how to do it! Above all, we should pray to fulfill the purpose for which God has put us in the earth; for true success is the degree to which we have done that.

---

[24] Eph. 4:1-6

ALSO BY THE AUTHOR

www.insightsfromthebible.com

Printed in the United States
by Baker & Taylor Publisher Services